CONTENTS

BE A WORD DETECTIVE

Can you find these words as you read about volcanoes? Be a detective and try to work out what they mean. You can turn to the glossary on page 46 for help.

ash	erupts	mantle
caldera	hot spots	plates
cinder cones	lahar	pyroclastic rocks
composite volcanoes	lava	shield volcanoes
crater	magma	vent
crust	magma chamber	volcanoes

CHAPTER 1
WHAT IS A VOLCANO?

Earth has many volcanoes. Some volcanoes are tall mountains. Some are huge holes in the ground. Others are hidden under the oceans.

Volcanoes are places where hot, molten (melted) rock comes out of the ground. Most rock is hard, but when rock gets very, very hot, it melts. Molten rock is soft. It flows slowly, like toothpaste being squeezed out of a tube.

Molten rock can be so hot that it glows yellow or red.

Deep inside the Earth, it is very hot. Some of the rock inside the Earth gets so hot that it melts. Molten rock that is inside the Earth is called magma. Magma has a small amount of gas mixed into it. The gas is mostly steam, which is the gas that forms when water boils.

Steam is coming out of this volcano.

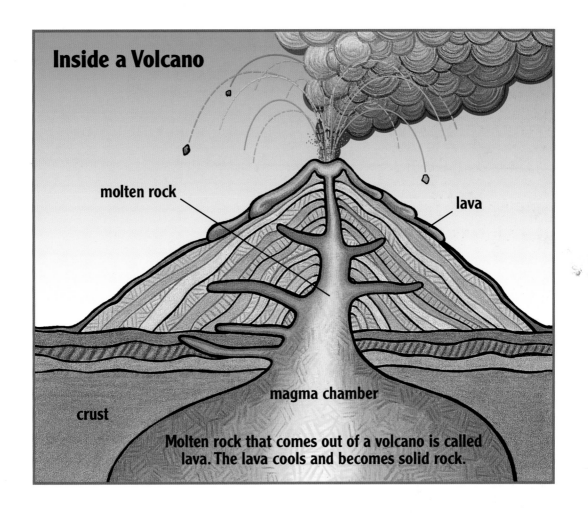

Inside a Volcano

molten rock

lava

magma chamber

crust

Molten rock that comes out of a volcano is called lava. The lava cools and becomes solid rock.

Magma moves around inside the Earth. Hot magma weighs less than most solid rock. Because it is lighter, magma rises through the cracks in solid rock. It fills up spaces in the rock. An underground space that is filled with magma is called a magma chamber.

Sometimes the magma pushes all the way to the Earth's surface. Then the magma erupts and spills out onto the surface. When magma flows onto the surface, it is called lava.

This volcano is under the Pacific Ocean. Red-hot lava is flowing across the ocean floor.

Lava is flowing from a vent inside this crater.

The opening from which lava flows is called a vent. A vent can be on the top or the side of a mountain, or on the ocean floor. Most vents are found inside craters. A crater is a hole shaped like a bowl.

Some lava is runny. Runny lava flows easily across the ground. Other lava is thicker and spreads more slowly.

This lava is very thick.

As lava cools, its colour becomes darker.

When lava comes out of a volcano, it cools and changes into solid rock. Some lava rock has a smooth surface. Other lava rock looks chunky and rough.

13

In some places, part of the Earth's rocky outer layer can be seen. What is this layer called?

CHAPTER 2

WHERE DO VOLCANOES FORM?

The Earth has three main layers, which are the core, the mantle and the crust. The core is the

Earth's centre. The mantle is the Earth's thick middle layer. The crust is the Earth's outer layer. We live on the Earth's crust.

The Earth's crust is usually hidden by soil and plants.

The mantle is very hot. Rock melts in some areas of the mantle because the temperature is so high. This rock becomes magma.

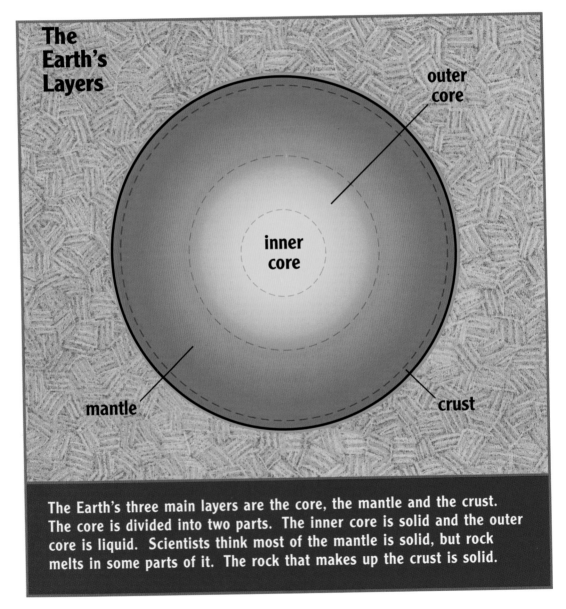

The Earth's Layers

outer core

inner core

mantle

crust

The Earth's three main layers are the core, the mantle and the crust. The core is divided into two parts. The inner core is solid and the outer core is liquid. Scientists think most of the mantle is solid, but rock melts in some parts of it. The rock that makes up the crust is solid.

Solid rock doesn't bend. If it is pushed hard enough, it breaks.

The crust is much cooler than the mantle. Rock
in the crust is solid. Solid rock cannot bend and
flow like magma.

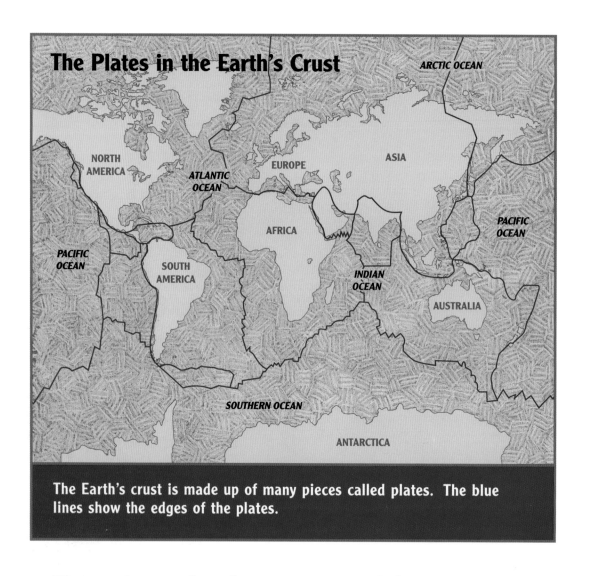

The Earth's crust is made up of many pieces called plates. The blue lines show the edges of the plates.

Huge pieces of rock cover most of the Earth's surface. They lie next to each other like the pieces of a jigsaw puzzle. These pieces of rock are called plates. The top of each plate is made of rock from the crust. The bottom of the plate is made of rock from the top of the mantle. The plates float on top of the rest of the mantle. In some places, plates slowly push and slide against each other. In other places, plates pull away from each other.

The Great Rift Valley is in Africa. The valley formed because two of the Earth's plates are slowly moving away from each other.

Most volcanoes form along the edges of the plates. When the plates push against each other or pull apart, rock gets squeezed or stretched. When the rock is squeezed or stretched, it becomes hot. Some of it melts and becomes magma. Wherever magma reaches the surface, a volcano forms.

Mount Fuji is a volcano in the country of Japan. Japan is near the edges of several of the Earth's plates.

Lanai is one of the Hawaiian Islands. The Hawaiian Islands formed above a hot spot in the middle of the Pacific Ocean.

Volcanoes can also form far away from a plate's edges. Rock in some areas of the mantle gets especially hot. Scientists call these areas hot spots. In hot spots, magma pushes upwards. It flows out of a vent and onto the surface.

The Hawaiian Islands are a chain of islands. They formed one by one above a hot spot in the Pacific Ocean. Magma erupted again and again into the water above the hot spot and the lava piled up higher and higher. After a long time, the lava rose above the water's surface. An island had formed. However, the plate beneath it was moving the whole time.

Seawater quickly cools lava that erupts underwater. The lava hardens into big lumps.

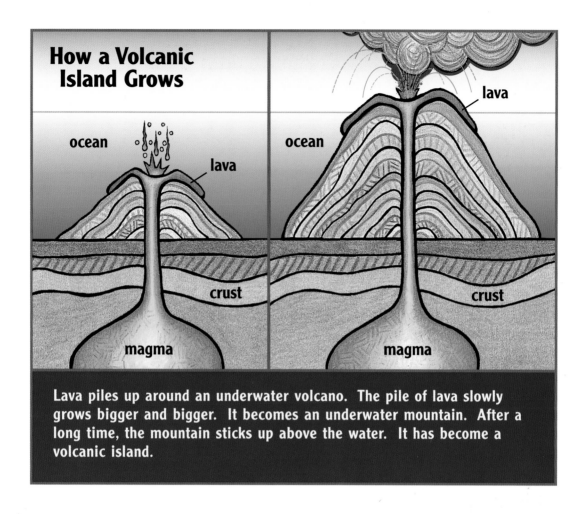

How a Volcanic Island Grows

ocean

lava

lava

ocean

crust

crust

magma

magma

Lava piles up around an underwater volcano. The pile of lava slowly grows bigger and bigger. It becomes an underwater mountain. After a long time, the mountain sticks up above the water. It has become a volcanic island.

Over many years, the plate carried the island away from the hot spot. Magma erupted from the hot spot again. A second island formed. Then that island was carried away from the hot spot. More and more islands formed as the plate kept moving.

CHAPTER 3
KINDS OF VOLCANOES

Some volcanoes have sides that are not very steep. These volcanoes look sort of like a warrior's shield lying on the ground. Scientists call them shield volcanoes.

Shield volcanoes form from lava that is runny, like syrup. Runny lava may flow for many kilometres before it cools and hardens. It covers the land like a huge blanket. Each time the volcano erupts, a new layer of lava is added on top of the old layers. As the layers pile up, they form a mountain that is shaped like a warrior's shield.

Mauna Kea is a shield volcano in Hawaii.

Some volcanoes are very tall and have steep sides. These volcanoes are called composite volcanoes. They form from thick lava. Thick lava doesn't flow very far before it starts to cool and harden. More lava is added during later eruptions, and the volcano becomes steeper and steeper. A tall, cone-shaped composite volcano gradually forms.

Mount Hood is a composite volcano in Oregon, in the USA.

This cinder cone is in New Zealand.

Cinder cones are small volcanoes with very steep sides. They form from magma that has a lot of gas bubbles in it. The bubbles explode when the magma flows out of a vent, and lava is thrown upwards. It cools as it flies through the air and becomes bits of solid rock. These rocks fall down around the vent. The pile of rock pieces gets taller each time the volcano erupts. Over time, the growing pile becomes a cinder cone.

These rocks are volcanic bombs.

Rocks that are thrown out of a volcano are called pyroclastic rocks. Large pyroclastic rocks are called bombs. Bombs are the size of a tennis ball or larger. Other pyroclastic rocks are very small. They look like large grains of sand. These pyroclastic rocks are called ash. Bombs fall to the ground like rain, but ash stays in the air longer. It can form huge clouds above a volcano.

Ash rises up from Mount Pinatubo, in the Philippines, during a volcanic eruption.

Sometimes very thick magma oozes from the vent in a volcano's crater. The lava piles up and becomes a lava dome. A lava dome looks like a tiny volcano inside a crater.

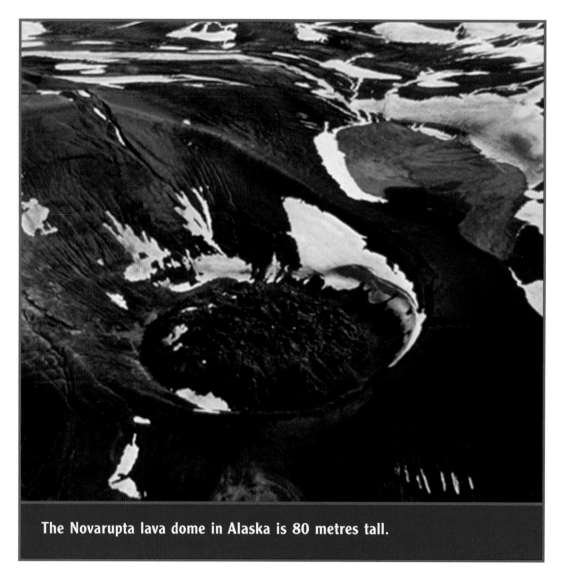

The Novarupta lava dome in Alaska is 80 metres tall.

Crater Lake is a caldera in Oregon, in the USA. The caldera is filled with water from melting snow.

After a volcano erupts, part of the magma chamber under it is left empty. Sometimes the rock above the chamber is so heavy that it falls down into the empty magma chamber. It makes a hole called a caldera. A caldera is much larger than a crater. Crater Lake in the USA is 10 km (6 miles) wide.

Basalt is a kind of lava rock. Where can basalt rock be found?

CHAPTER 4

ROCKS FROM VOLCANOES

When lava comes out of a volcano, it cools and hardens and becomes solid rock. Different kinds of lava become different types of rock.

32

One kind of lava rock is called basalt. The lava that erupts from volcanoes above hot spots usually hardens into basalt. The top of the Earth's crust under the oceans is made of basalt.

Andesite is a type of lava rock that forms from thick magma. It forms in places where one of the Earth's plates slides under another.

Andesite was named after the Andes Mountains in South America.

Some magma is filled with lots of gas bubbles. This sort of magma looks foamy. When foamy magma cools quickly, it becomes a type of rock called pumice. Pumice is filled with tiny air bubbles, or holes. Air doesn't weigh much. The air inside pumice makes it weigh less than other kinds of rock. In fact, pumice can be so light that it floats in water.

Pumice rock is full of holes.

Most obsidian rock is black.

Sometimes lava cools very quickly. When this happens, it becomes a type of lava rock called obsidian. Obsidian looks like dark, shiny glass. It is smooth to touch, but when it breaks, it has very sharp edges.

Hot lava from a volcano set this house on fire. What is another way that volcanoes can be dangerous?

CHAPTER 5

VOLCANOES AND PEOPLE

Hot lava is dangerous. It can burn buildings and kill people and animals. However, because most lava flows slowly, people can usually see the lava coming and can get away from it.

Some volcanoes are much more dangerous than flowing lava. A big cloud of ash and rock may rush down the sides of a volcano. The cloud is called a pyroclastic flow. The flow is burning hot and buries everything in its path. People cannot run fast enough to escape a pyroclastic flow. Many people may be killed.

Mount Saint Helens, in the USA, erupted in 1980. A cloud of ash and rock rushed down the side of the mountain.

Some volcanoes are tall mountains. Their tops are covered with snow and ice. When these volcanoes erupt, heat from magma melts the snow. The snow becomes water. The water runs down the mountain. As it flows, it mixes with soil and rocks to make mud. The flowing mud is called a lahar. The lahar gushes down the sides of the volcano. It knocks down trees, buildings and huge rocks.

These houses were buried by rocks and sand that came from a volcano.

Some volcanoes make huge clouds of ash.

Wind can carry ash far from an erupting volcano. Some ash may be blown thousands of kilometres. Blowing ash is dangerous. If a plane flies through an ash cloud, the ash gets sucked into the plane's engines. It makes the engines stop working and the plane may crash.

Volcanoes can change the weather too. Heat from the sun warms up the air. A big ash cloud can block sunlight, in the same way that rain clouds do. When ash blocks sunlight, the Earth's air does not get as warm.

Rain clouds block sunlight. Ash from a volcano blocks sunlight too.

The Earth's mantle is deep underground, so scientists can't look at it. To find out more about the mantle, scientists study lava from volcanoes. The lava started out as magma in the Earth's mantle.

Scientists study volcanoes to find out if they might erupt. Sometimes the ground shakes near a volcano. It shakes because magma is moving far beneath the volcano. When the ground shakes a lot, the volcano may be about to erupt. Then scientists warn people who live nearby and tell them to go to a safer place.

Volcanoes can be dangerous, but they can also help people. Over time, lava rocks break apart. The pieces of rock become part of the soil. Plants grow very well in soil that has lava rock in it.

Hawaii's soil has bits of lava rock in it. Plants grow well in this soil.

Look around your area. What types of rocks can you find?

Studying rocks made by volcanoes is fun. Can you find rocks such as basalt, andesite, obsidian or pumice where you live? Even if no volcanoes are in your area now, one might have been there millions of years ago. Be a volcano detective and see what you can find.

LEARN MORE ABOUT
VOLCANOES

BOOKS

Farndon, John. *Volcanoes and Earthquakes* (Bulletpoints) Miles Kelly Publishing Limited, 2003.

Greenwood, Rosie. *I Wonder Why Volcanoes Blow Their Tops and Other Questions About Natural Disasters* (I Wonder Why) Kingfisher Books, 2004.

Hunter, Rebecca. *Volcanoes and Earthquakes* (Discovering Geography) Raintree Publishers, 2004.

Mayer, Cassie. *Volcanoes* (Landforms) Heinemann, 2006.

Putnam, James and Susanna Van Rose. *Volcano* (Eyewitness) Dorling Kindersley Publishers Limited, 2002.

WEBSITES

BBC – Animated Guide to Volcanoes
http://news.bbc.co.uk/1/hi/sci/tech/4972366.stm
This animation shows how and why a volcano erupts and will help you to explore some of the Earth's major volcanoes.

CBBC Newsround – Volcanoes
http://news.bbc.co.uk/cbbcnews/hi/find_out/guides/tech/volcanoes/newsid_1768000/1768595.stm
Use this website to find out more about volcanoes and to learn some interesting facts.

Natural History Museum – Natural Disasters
http://www.nhm.ac.uk/nature-online/earth/volcanoes-earthquakes/index.html
Find out about the different kinds of natural disasters that affect the Earth. This website includes a section about volcanoes and a video of a volcanic eruption.

GLOSSARY

ash: small rocks thrown out of volcanoes

caldera: a hole in the ground that forms when the rock above a magma chamber falls down

cinder cones: small volcanoes with very steep sides

composite volcanoes: tall volcanoes with steep sides

crater: a hole in the ground that is shaped like a bowl

crust: the Earth's outer layer. We live on the Earth's crust.

erupts: spills out onto the Earth's surface

hot spots: places in the Earth's mantle that are hotter than the rest of the mantle

lahar: hot mud that flows quickly down the sides of a volcano

lava: molten rock on the Earth's surface

magma: molten rock that is inside the Earth

magma chamber: an underground space that is filled with molten rock

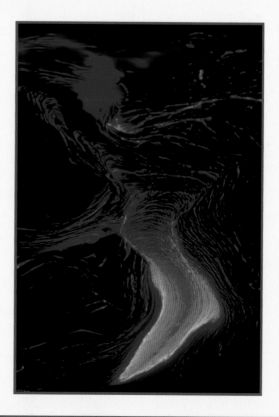

mantle: the Earth's thick middle layer. The mantle is on top of the core and under the crust.

plates: huge pieces of rock that cover the Earth's surface like the pieces of a puzzle

pyroclastic rocks: rocks thrown out of a volcano

shield volcanoes: volcanoes whose sides are not steep

vent: an opening from which lava flows

volcanoes: places where hot, molten rock comes out of the ground

INDEX

Pages listed in **bold** refer to photographs.

First published in the United States of America in 2008
Text copyright © 2008 by Sally M Walker